Meet My Pet

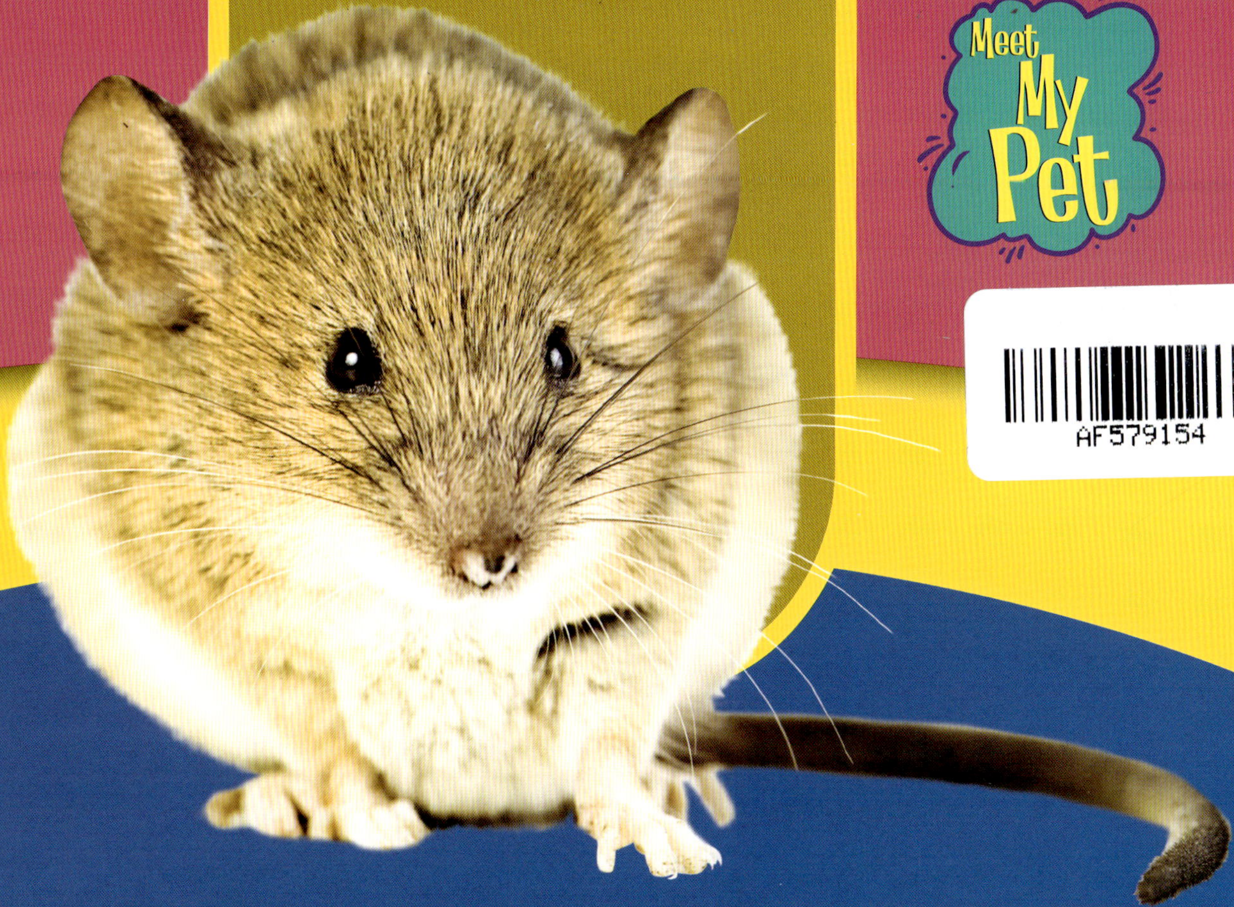

MOUSE

Lydia Lukidis

AV2
www.openlightbox.com

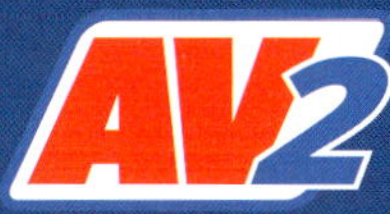

Step 1
Go to **www.openlightbox.com**

Step 2
Enter this unique code
RGQUXF0VN

Step 3
Explore your interactive eBook!

Meet My Pet
AV2
MOUSE
Start!
Share

AV2 is optimized for use on any device

Your interactive eBook comes with...

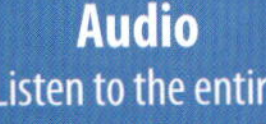
Audio Listen to the entire book read aloud

Videos Watch informative video clips

Weblinks Gain additional information for research

Try This! Complete activities and hands-on experiments

Key Words Study vocabulary, and complete a matching word activity

Quizzes Test your knowledge

Slideshows View images and captions

Share Share titles within your Learning Management System (LMS) or Library Circulation System

Citation Create bibliographical references following APA, CMOS, and MLA styles

This title is part of our AV2 digital subscription

1-Year K–5 Subscription
ISBN 978-1-7911-3320-7

Access hundreds of AV2 titles with our digital subscription.
Sign up for a FREE trial at www.openlightbox.com/trial

The digital components of this book are guaranteed to stay active for at least five years from the date of publication.

MOUSE

CONTENTS

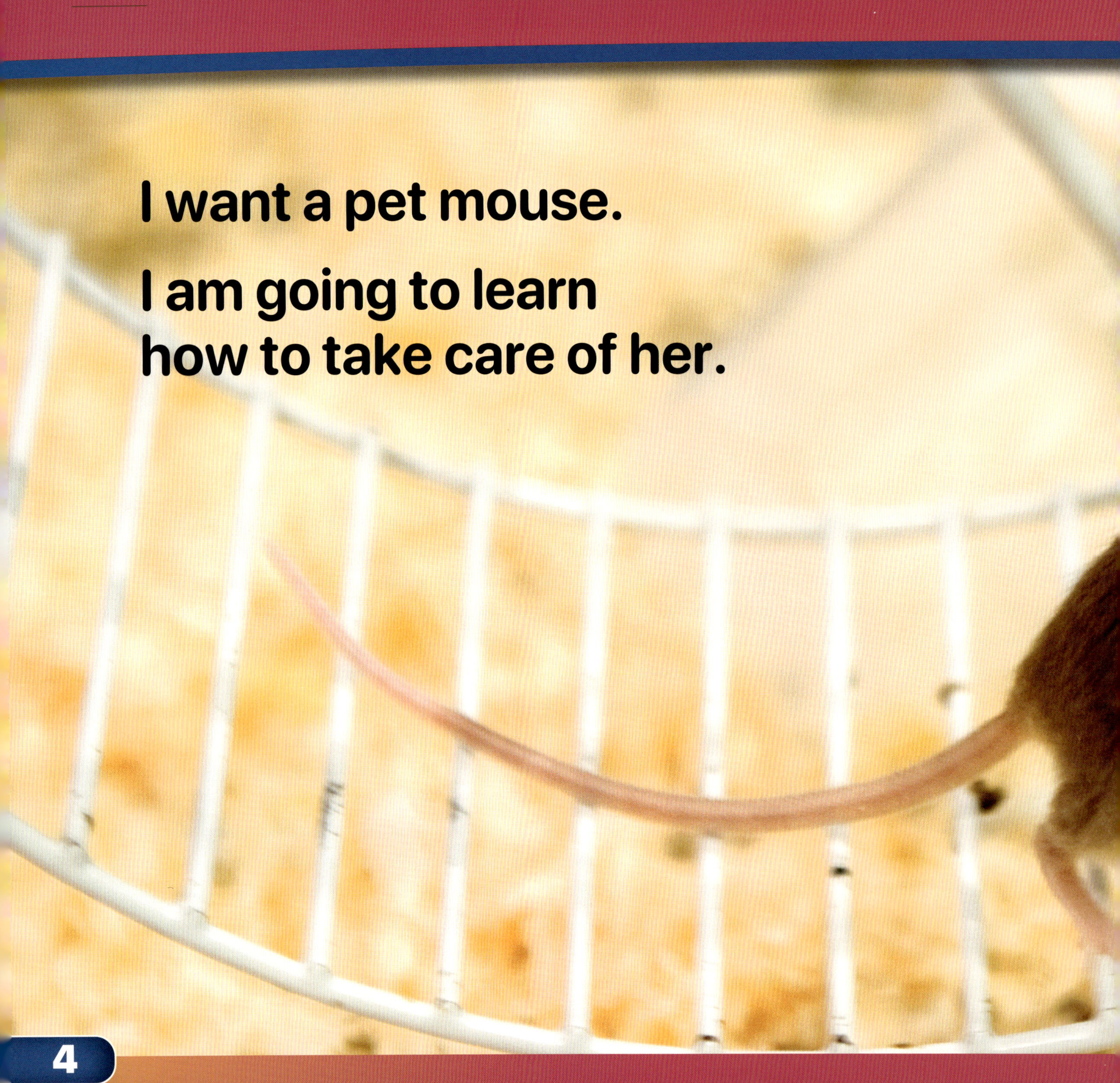

I want a pet mouse.

I am going to learn how to take care of her.

I can choose from many kinds of mice.

Mice can have different types of fur.

MOUSE FUR

Hairless 
Astrex 
Standard

Texel

Mice like to stay clean.

They clean themselves many times a day.

Mice have long, thin tails.

Their tails help them stand up straight and run fast.

PET TAIL LENGTH

Mouse

Up to **4** inches (10 centimeters) long

Ferret

About **5** inches (13 cm) long

Cat

About **12** inches (30 cm) long

Dog

8 to **16** inches (20 to 41 cm) long

Mice are friendly and
like to be with people.

I will pet my mouse
and feed her treats.

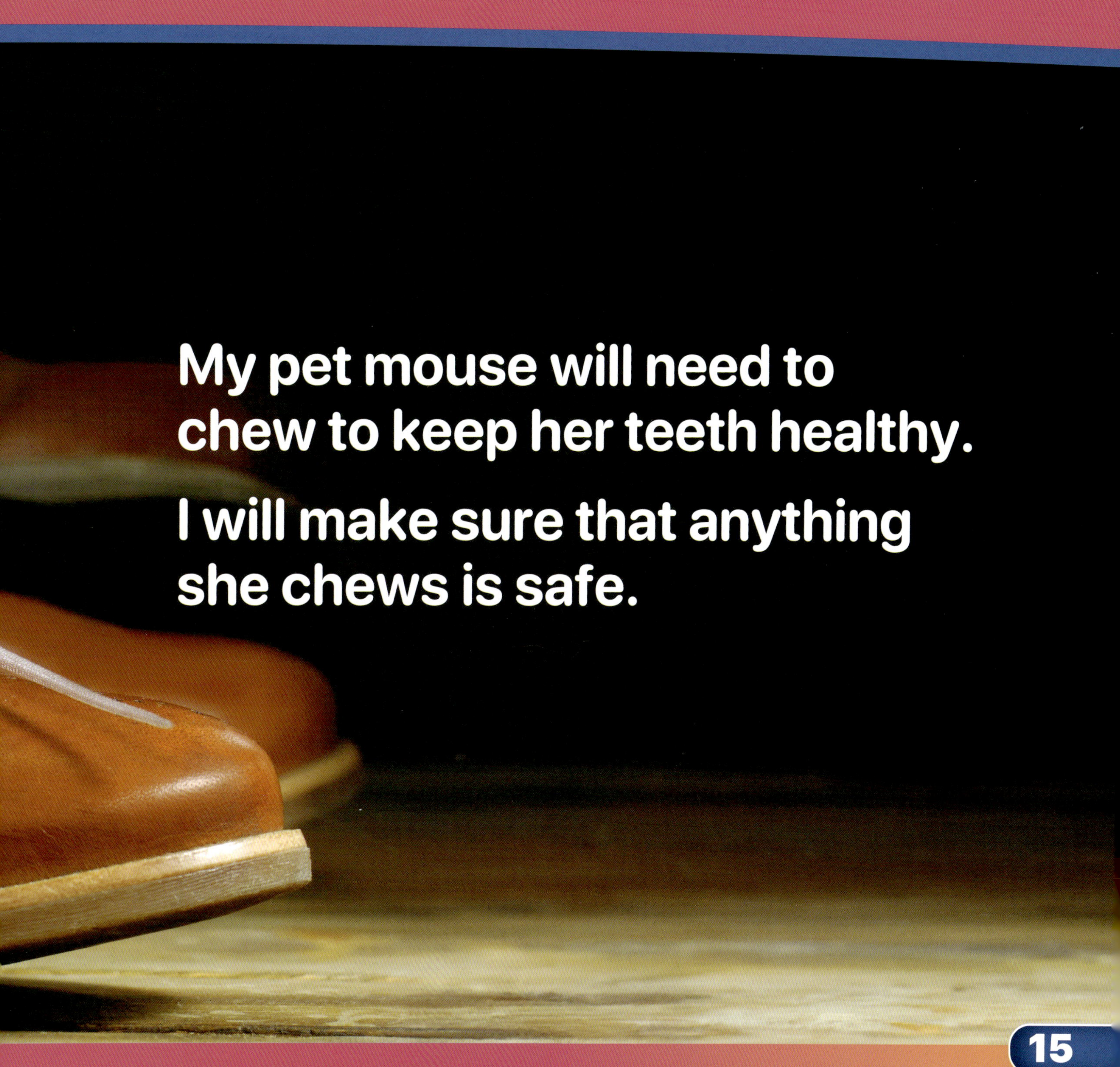

My pet mouse will need to chew to keep her teeth healthy.

I will make sure that anything she chews is safe.

I will feed my pet mouse every day.

She will eat many types of food.

My pet mouse will spend most of her time in her cage.

She will sleep during the day. She will be most active at night.

GROWING UP

Newborn Pup

0.02 to 0.05 ounces (0.6 to 1.4 grams)
She has no fur. Her eyes are closed.
She drinks her mother's milk.

3-Week-Old Mouse

0.3 to 0.4 ounces (8.5 to 11 g)
Her hair has grown.
She eats solid food.

8-Week-Old Mouse

0.6 to 0.8 ounces (17 to 23 g)
She is curious and likes to explore.
She can have babies.

6-Month-Old Mouse

0.9 to 1.8 ounces (26 to 51 g)
She stops growing.
She sleeps 12 hours a day.

I love my pet mouse.

I will take good care of her.

THINK ABOUT IT!

What other steps can you take to keep your mouse happy and healthy?

MOUSE FACTS

These pages provide detailed information that expands on the interesting facts found in the book. They are intended to be used by adults as a learning support to help young readers round out their knowledge of each amazing animal featured in the *Meet My Pet* series.

Pages 4–5

I want a pet mouse. Scientists believe that mice began to live alongside humans about 15,000 years ago in the Middle East. When people stopped hunting and gathering to settle down in homes, mice slowly crept into those homes for food and shelter. By the 1700s, many varieties of mice were kept as pets in China and Japan. From there, they arrived in Great Britain, where "fancy" mice became very popular pets in the Victorian era.

Pages 6–7

I can choose from many kinds of mice. There are 38 species of mice. Pet mice come from house mice (*Mus musculus*) and can have several different types of coats. When choosing a pet mouse, it is important to select a domesticated mouse from an expert breeder. Non-domesticated mice can be dangerous and should not be kept in captivity. They are not tamed and may carry dangerous infections or diseases.

Pages 8–9

Mice like to stay clean. Owners do not need to bathe or groom their pet mice. These animals can spend up to 40 percent of their waking hours self-grooming. They do this by licking dirt from their fur. Responsible owners can help their pet mice stay clean by removing all droppings from their cages and changing their bedding regularly.

Pages 10–11

Mice have long, thin tails. Most mice have tails that are nearly as long as their bodies. The tail has many functions. It maintains the mouse's balance and center of gravity. This allows the animal to stand on its hind legs without falling over. The tail also helps a mouse maintain a healthy body temperature. A mouse can survive without a tail, but it will be more vulnerable to predators. It will not be as agile or run as fast as it would with a tail.

Pages 12–13

Mice are friendly and like to be with people. Petting and snuggling with a pet mouse is possible with some precautions. A mouse may bite when scared. Owners need to make sure not to startle their pet when handling it. People should be especially careful when holding mice, as their skeletons are very fragile. Young children in particular should be supervised when handling mice. It is recommended that owners slowly develop a bond with their pet. This can be done by allowing it to become accustomed to human presence before attempting to handle it.

Pages 14–15

My pet mouse will need to chew to keep her teeth healthy. A mouse's largest teeth are its incisors, or front teeth. Mice use these teeth for self-defence, to dig burrows, and to chew their food. The incisors never stop growing. Mice need to constantly chew and gnaw on objects such as toys and objects made out of wood. Chewing helps them wear down their teeth and keep them at a reasonable length. Owners should pay attention and prevent their mice from chewing on dangerous items, such as electric cables.

Pages 16–17

I will feed my pet mouse every day. Mice should be fed high-quality rodent pellets daily. Mice like to graze when awake. Veterinarians recommend that owners keep a small ceramic bowl in their pet's cage, filled with enough food for one day. As a treat, mice can eat seeds and grains, as well as fresh fruit and vegetables such as apples, carrots, and broccoli. These should be cut into small, bite-sized pieces. Mice also need access to fresh water. A bottle attached to their cage will provide them with an easily accessible supply.

Pages 18–19

My pet mouse will spend most of her time in her cage. Pet mice should live and sleep in an enclosed habitat, such as a cage. The cage needs to be well-ventilated and secured with an escape-proof lid. Wire cages provide the best ventilation and are easy to clean. Glass and plastic terrariums are not recommended because their solid walls block air circulation. Mice are nocturnal. This means that they are generally more active at night and sleep throughout the day. They need about 12 hours of sleep daily.

Pages 20–21

I love my pet mouse. Mice are social animals. Ideally, people should adopt more than one mouse at the time. Mice also need exercise to stay healthy. An exercise wheel can provide them with hours of entertainment. To rest comfortably, mice need bedding at least 1 inch (2.5 cm) thick, in the form of wood shavings or shredded filter paper.

KEY WORDS

Research has shown that as much as 65 percent of all written material published in English is made up of 300 words. These 300 words cannot be taught using pictures or learned by sounding them out. They must be recognized by sight. This book contains 60 common sight words to help young readers improve their reading fluency and comprehension. This book also teaches young readers several important content words, such as proper nouns. These words are paired with pictures to aid in learning and improve understanding.

Page	Sight Words First Appearance
4	a, am, her, how, I, learn, of, take, to, want
6	can, different, from, kinds, have, many
8	day, like, they, times
10	and, help, long, run, their, them, up
11	about
12	are, be, my, people, will, with
15	is, keep, make, need, she, that
16	eat, every, food
18	at, in, most, night, the
19	has, eyes, mother, no, stops
20	good
21	it, other, think, what, you, your

Page	Content Words First Appearance
4	mouse
6	fur, types
7	astrex, hairless, standard, texel
10	tails
11	cat, dog, ferret, length
12	treats
15	teeth
18	cage
19	babies, hair, milk, newborn pup
21	steps

Published by Lightbox Learning Inc.
276 5th Avenue, Suite 704 #917
New York, NY 10001
Website: www.openlightbox.com

Library of Congress Control Number available upon request.

ISBN 979-8-8745-0583-7 (hardcover)
ISBN 979-8-8745-0584-4 (softcover)
ISBN 979-8-8745-0965-1 (static multi-user eBook)
ISBN 979-8-8745-0585-1 (interactive multi-user eBook)

Printed in Guangzhou, China
1 2 3 4 5 6 7 8 9 0 28 27 26 25 24

042024
100923

Project Coordinator: Sara Cucini **Art Director:** Terry Paulhus

Every reasonable effort has been made to trace ownership and to obtain permission to reprint copyright material. The publisher would be pleased to have any errors or omissions brought to its attention so that they may be corrected in subsequent printings.

The publisher acknowledges Getty Images and Shutterstock as the primary image suppliers for this title.